# Who Is
# Neil Armstrong?

# Who Is
# Neil Armstrong?

By Roberta Edwards
Illustrated by Stephen Marchesi

Grosset & Dunlap

For my father and to those for whom
the journey is the destination.—S.M.

GROSSET & DUNLAP
Published by the Penguin Group
Penguin Group (USA) Inc., 375 Hudson Street, New York, New York 10014, USA
Penguin Group (Canada), 90 Eglinton Avenue East, Suite 700, Toronto, Ontario
M4P 2Y3, Canada (a division of Pearson Penguin Canada Inc.)
Penguin Books Ltd., 80 Strand, London WC2R 0RL, England
Penguin Group Ireland, 25 St. Stephen's Green, Dublin 2, Ireland
(a division of Penguin Books Ltd.)
Penguin Group (Australia), 250 Camberwell Road, Camberwell, Victoria 3124, Australia
(a division of Pearson Australia Group Pty. Ltd.)
Penguin Books India Pvt. Ltd., 11 Community Centre, Panchsheel Park,
New Delhi—110 017, India
Penguin Group (NZ), 67 Apollo Drive, Rosedale, North Shore 0632, New Zealand (a
division of Pearson New Zealand Ltd.)
Penguin Books (South Africa) (Pty.) Ltd., 24 Sturdee Avenue,
Rosebank, Johannesburg 2196, South Africa

Penguin Books Ltd., Registered Offices: 80 Strand, London WC2R 0RL, England

Text copyright © 2008 by Grosset & Dunlap.
Illustrations copyright © 2008 by Stephen Marchesi.
Cover illustration copyright © 2008 by Nancy Harrison.
Published by Grosset & Dunlap,
a division of Penguin Young Readers Group,
345 Hudson Street, New York, New York 10014.
GROSSET & DUNLAP is a trademark of Penguin Group (USA) Inc.
Printed in the U.S.A.

Library of Congress Control Number: 2008010691

ISBN 978-0-448-44907-4          20  19  18  17  16  15  14

# Contents

# Who Is
# Neil Armstrong?

It is July 16, 1969. By 9 A.M. the temperature hits a whopping ninety degrees. That's just a typical summer morning in central Florida. The heat does not stop a crowd of a million people from coming as close to Cape Kennedy as they can get. That is where the United States will launch a spacecraft in just a little while. Carloads of people line the roads for miles. Hundreds of boats bob in the waters just offshore. The beaches swarm with people. Everyone hopes to get a glimpse of the *Apollo 11* spacecraft as it soars off into the heavens.

Two thousand reporters are in the press area, ready to write headline stories for their newspapers. In special stands nearest to the launchpad at Cape Kennedy are many members of Congress, the U.S.

vice president, and many famous names in show business and sports.

Among all these important people are two young boys, twelve-year-old Rick and six-year-old Mark Armstrong. They stand close to their mother, Janet, who looks as nervous and excited as they do.

Like everyone else, the boys are watching the giant needlelike rocket. It stands thirty stories high.

At the very top is a space capsule; three astronauts are inside. One of them is the boys' father. His name

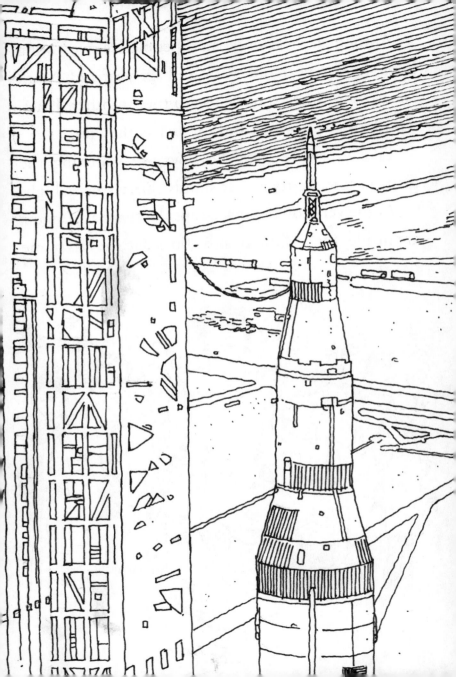

is Neil Armstrong. He is the commander of this space mission—*Apollo 11*. And if all goes well, in four days he will become the first person to set foot on the moon . . . but that is a big *if.* No spacecraft has ever tried to land on the moon before. What if *Apollo 11* makes it to the moon but then can't get back to Earth? . . . So many things could go wrong.

*Apollo 11* may either make history or end in tragedy.

# Chapter 1
# A Boy Who Loved Flying

Just after midnight on August 5, 1930, Neil Armstrong was born in the Ohio farmhouse that belonged to his grandparents.

Neil was the oldest of Stephen and Viola Armstrong's three children. He had a younger sister named June and a younger brother named Dean. Neil was always his mother's pet. She once

wrote that he was "a pleasure for us to raise" in every way. Maybe that was because Neil was a lot like his mother—calm, serious, and determined. Neil never had trouble making friends. Still, he was shy and not as fun-loving as Dean.

Neil's mother stayed at home caring for the children. She also taught Sunday school. Neil's father worked for the Ohio state government. Because of his job, the family had to move many times—in fact, they moved sixteen times before Neil was thirteen! Finally the Armstrongs settled in the little Ohio town of Wapakoneta.

In the 1930s planes were still thought of as unusual—and exciting. Many people had never flown in one. Only three years before Neil was born, in 1927, Charles Lindbergh flew nonstop across the Atlantic. He was the first person to make a transatlantic flight, and it took thirty-three and a half hours! To get to Europe, people from the United States still traveled by ship, which took four days on a luxury liner. For long trips across the country, people took trains. In 1930 it took about a week to get from New York to California by railroad.

From the time he was a little boy, Neil was fascinated by airplanes and flying. When he was just a toddler, he saw an air show in Cleveland, Ohio, with his dad. Neil took his first plane ride when he was only six. The plane was called the *Tin Goose*. It wasn't really made out of tin. Its strong body was made of aluminum. The *Tin Goose* could carry up to twelve passengers, who sat on

scratchy wicker seats. Its engines rattled and roared
as "the goose" reached a little over a hundred
miles an hour. Later on, Neil's father
confessed that he had been
"scared to death." As for
Neil, he had enjoyed
every minute.

*Tin Goose*

# THE FIRST AIRPLANE

THE WRIGHT BROTHERS, ORVILLE AND WILBUR, GREW UP IN DAYTON, OHIO, NEAR WHERE NEIL ARMSTRONG WAS BORN. LIKE NEIL, THEY WERE INTERESTED IN ANYTHING THAT FLEW FROM THE TIME THEY WERE KIDS. THEY MADE PAPER TOYS THAT THEY CALLED BATS, WHICH COULD GLIDE ON AIR CURRENTS.

BUT IN 1903, WHEN WILBUR WAS THIRTY-SIX AND ORVILLE WAS THIRTY-TWO, THEY DID SOMETHING AMAZING, SOMETHING THAT PEOPLE HAD DREAMED OF DOING FOR THOUSANDS OF YEARS. THEY BUILT THE FIRST REAL AIRPLANE—ONE WITH AN ENGINE—THAT ACTUALLY FLEW INSTEAD OF GLIDING ON THE WIND.

THEIR ONE-SEATER PLANE WAS MADE OF WOOD AND CLOTH. IT WAS EIGHT FEET HIGH AND HAD WINGS THAT WENT FORTY FEET ACROSS. ORVILLE MADE THE FIRST SUCCESSFUL FLIGHT ON DECEMBER 17, 1903, IN KITTY HAWK, NORTH CAROLINA. (THE WEATHER WAS MUCH BETTER THERE THAN IN OHIO!)

HOW LONG WAS THE FLIGHT? ONLY TWELVE SECONDS.

AND HOW FAR DID THE PLANE TRAVEL? ONLY 120 FEET. AND IT WAS ONLY TWENTY FEET OFF THE GROUND. BUT IT WAS THE BEGINNING OF A WHOLE NEW AGE!

Neil loved building model planes out of balsa wood, wire, and tissue paper. They were powered by wound-up rubber bands. In the basement, he set up a wind tunnel with a fan so he could see how well his models flew. According to his brother Dean, sometimes Neil would fly one of his old model planes out the window. He thought it was exciting to watch it crash on the driveway.

Neil belonged to a Boy Scout troop for many years. In fact, Neil became an Eagle Scout, the highest level in scouting. It was the 1940s by this time, and the United States was fighting against Germany in World War II. Neil and the other scouts made models of different enemy planes. No warplanes ever came anywhere near Ohio. Still, if one had, Neil could have identified it right away!

Neil read airplane magazines; he drew detailed sketches of his favorite planes. Learning about planes, however, wasn't the same as learning to fly planes. And that's what Neil wanted to do most of all.

# THE FIRST FLIGHT ACROSS THE ATLANTIC

ON MAY 20, 1927, A YOUNG PILOT NAMED CHARLES LINDBERGH SET OUT FROM LONG ISLAND ALL BY HIMSELF IN A SMALL, SINGLE-ENGINE PLANE TO CROSS THE ATLANTIC OCEAN. IT WAS CALLED THE *SPIRIT OF ST. LOUIS*. THE TRIP WAS DARING AND DANGEROUS. LINDBERGH HAD NO RADIO OR PARACHUTE. THERE WAS JUST ENOUGH ROOM IN THE COCKPIT FOR HIM TO SIT WITH HIS LEGS BENT.

IN PARIS, THIRTY-THREE HOURS LATER, 100,000 PEOPLE WERE WAITING TO GREET CHARLES LINDBERGH. OVERNIGHT HE BECAME THE MOST FAMOUS MAN ON EARTH, AS FAMOUS AS NEIL ARMSTRONG WOULD BECOME A LITTLE MORE THAN FORTY YEARS LATER.

## Chapter 2
## Real Planes

Neil was determined to fly. Port Koneta airfield was nearby. (Today it's the Wapakoneta Neil Armstrong Airport.) As a teenager Neil took part-time jobs to pay for flying lessons.

He mowed the lawn at a cemetery. He helped bake doughnuts at a doughnut company—more than 1,300 a night. He got the job at the doughnut

company because he was small enough to climb inside the dough mixer and clean it! All this extra money went to flying lessons. By the time Neil was fifteen, he had earned his pilot's license. Now he knew how to fly a plane, but he was still too young to drive!

At Blume High School, only six blocks from his home, Neil wasn't a top student. But he was better than average. Like his mother, he was musical. He played baritone horn in a jazz band called the Mississippi Moonshiners.

From the time he learned to read, he loved books. In his first year of elementary school he read more than a hundred! In high school, his favorite subjects were science and math. He wanted to go on to college; he wanted to learn more about planes and how they flew.

The Armstrongs were not poor. They owned their home; they had a car; there was always enough food. But money was still tight. And a college education was very expensive. Neil, however, was able to attend Purdue University in Indiana on a Navy scholarship. He wanted to study aeronautic engineering—how planes are built and what makes them fly. In return for the scholarship money, Neil had to serve in the U.S. Navy.

This arrangement was fine with Neil. In the Navy, he could fly planes!

# Chapter 3
# The Wider World

When Neil started college, he had just turned seventeen. For the first time he was living away from his family. He got decent grades, as he had in high school. But he wasn't focused on his studies, and the science classes were hard. He described his freshman year as "kind of a whirl."

After two years at Purdue came three years in the Navy. This was when Neil Armstrong became an airman. He was stationed in Pensacola, Florida, where he learned to fly small, single-engine fighter planes.

# CHUCK YEAGER

CHARLES (CHUCK) YEAGER ALSO LOVED FLYING. DURING WORLD WAR II HE WAS A DARING PILOT WHO SHOT DOWN ENEMY PLANES. AFTER THE END OF THE WAR IN 1945, HE WORKED TESTING EXPERIMENTAL PLANES. SCIENTISTS AND ENGINEERS WANTED TO DESIGN A PLANE THAT COULD GO FASTER THAN THE SPEED OF SOUND. (THAT'S ABOUT 761 MILES AN HOUR.)

BY THE LATE 1940S, A NEW PLANE, CALLED THE BELL X-1, HAD BEEN DEVELOPED. YEAGER WAS CHOSEN TO PILOT IT ON ITS FIRST FLIGHT. EVEN A HORSEBACK RIDING ACCIDENT TWO NIGHTS BEFORE THE FLIGHT DIDN'T STOP HIM. FEARING THAT A DOCTOR WOULD TELL HIS BOSSES THAT HE WASN'T FIT TO FLY, YEAGER WENT TO A VET WHO BANDAGED UP HIS BROKEN RIBS. ONLY A MONTH AFTER NEIL ARMSTRONG STARTED COLLEGE, CHUCK YEAGER GOT INTO THE COCKPIT OF THE X-1 AND BROKE THE SOUND BARRIER DURING A FOURTEEN-MINUTE FLIGHT. (THERE ISN'T ACTUALLY A REAL BARRIER TO BREAK, BUT THE TERM IS STILL USED.)

At Pensacola the training began with twenty short flights called "hops." The instructor sat up front. Neil sat behind and had to pilot the plane even though it was harder to see from the back. Neil was graded on every hop. After that Neil went on to fly solo. He also took courses in aeronautic engineering as he had at Purdue.

He graduated and earned his "wings" pin from flight training school in August of 1950. Now

he was a licensed Navy aviator, and he was only twenty years old. He still had two years left at Purdue. However, Neil did not return to college as planned.

Why?

War had broken out—the Korean War, a war that lasted three years. The war sent Neil Armstrong halfway across the globe.

# THE KOREAN WAR

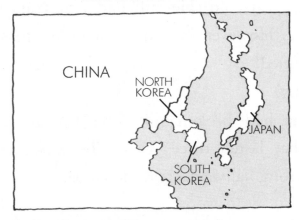

THE KOREAN PENINSULA JUTS OUT INTO THE PACIFIC OCEAN. NORTH KOREA HAS A COMMUNIST GOVERNMENT, WHILE SOUTH KOREA IS A DEMOCRACY. THE WAR BEGAN IN 1950 AFTER NORTH KOREA INVADED SOUTH KOREA.

RIGHT AWAY, AMERICAN TROOPS WENT TO SOUTH KOREA'S AID. MANY OTHER COUNTRIES IN THE UNITED NATIONS ALSO JOINED THE U.S. EFFORT. COMMUNIST CHINA AND THE U.S.S.R., HOWEVER, SENT SOLDIERS TO HELP NORTH KOREAN FORCES.

THE FIGHTING LASTED FOR THREE YEARS. FINALLY THE TWO SIDES AGREED TO A CEASE-FIRE IN JULY OF 1953. TODAY, AS THEN, THERE IS STILL NORTH KOREA AND SOUTH KOREA.

In Korea, Neil Armstrong belonged to Fighter Squadron 51. He was one of the very youngest pilots. The squadron flew small jets off a giant aircraft carrier called the USS *Essex*. Neil's job was to bomb enemy bridges and railroad lines or scout areas where other planes would attack later on. To

USS *Essex*

do this, Neil's plane had to fly very low and close to the ground. During the Korean War, Neil flew on seventy-eight missions. It was a dangerous and stressful job. But Neil Armstrong never lost his cool.

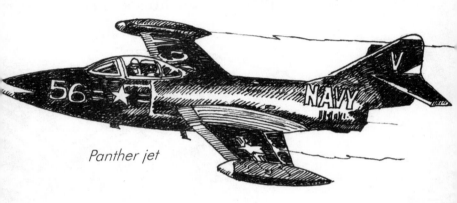

*Panther jet*

On one mission, Neil was in his Panther jet plane making a low bombing run in a hilly area of Korea. Suddenly his plane was hit by enemy gunfire. Neil lost control as the craft took a nosedive, hurtling toward the ground. At five hundred feet, part of the right wing was sheared off by a cable strung across the valley as a booby trap. Luckily, Neil regained control of the plane again and flew back to friendly territory. But the plane was too badly damaged to land. Neil had to bail out of the plane. His silk parachute billowed out, and he landed safely in a rice paddy. Two days later he was back aboard the aircraft carrier. Except for a cracked tailbone, Neil was unhurt.

Almost 34,000 Americans were killed in the Korean War, but Neil Armstrong returned home with many medals. Now it was time to finish up college and receive his diploma.

# Chapter 4
# Test Pilot

Neil had been younger than nearly all the other students when he first enrolled at Purdue. But he'd been away for three years. When he returned in September of 1952, he was twenty-two and older than most students. He was more mature. He was

ready to study harder. During his last two years at Purdue, his grades improved greatly. He also joined a fraternity and—for the very first time—fell in love.

Her name was Janet Shearon. Everyone called her Jan. She was an eighteen-year-old freshman at Purdue. Whereas Neil was quiet, Jan was outgoing. She loved being around people. She and Neil were married in 1956, several months after his graduation. Neil's hope was to become an

experimental test pilot. Not only would he get to fly new types of aircraft, but he would help figure out ways to build better planes.

At Edwards Air Force Base in the Mojave Desert of California, the newest planes were first tried out. Naturally, Neil wanted to work there.

So he and Jan moved to California. This meant Jan had to leave Purdue without finishing her degree. But Neil's career came first.

At Edwards Air Force Base, one of the planes Neil flew was called the X-15. It was rocket propelled. Instead of taking off from an airstrip, it had to be launched from another plane already in flight. The X-15 could go nearly 4,000 miles an hour and reach an altitude of 207,500 feet. (Today, regular passenger jets travel at about six hundred miles an hour, at an altitude of about 40,000 feet.)

The X-15 was flying fifty miles above the Earth.

That altitude is considered the start of outer space. So flying the X-15 was an early test for flying into space.

Neil said, "We were using airplanes as tools to gather all kinds of information, just as an astronomer uses a telescope as a tool. We didn't fly often, but when we did, it was unbelievably exciting."

Even when Neil was on the ground, he lived high up in the San Gabriel Mountains. He and Jan bought a little cabin, far from town. It didn't even have hot water. Sometimes Neil would fly by in a small plane and

Jan would wave out the window.

Jan, who was an expert swimmer, taught lifesaving classes to children. She and Neil also wanted to have a family of their own. In 1957, their first child, Eric, was born. His parents called him Rick. Two years later, in 1959, the Armstrongs had a little girl. Her name was Karen. But Neil gave her a nickname, too. It was Muffie. Neil was especially close to his little daughter, who was a sweet and happy child.

Then in the summer of 1961, two-year-old Muffie fell and hit her head on a sidewalk. It

wasn't a bad accident. Yet, afterward, her eyes became crossed. She started to run fevers. She tripped all the time. Her parents took her to a doctor right away. The news was terrible—Muffie had cancer. There was a tumor deep inside her brain.

Today there are so many medicines to treat cancer; unfortunately many of them were not discovered until after Muffie became sick. Doctors did everything they could to make her well. She lived through Christmas but died at home with her family on a Sunday morning in January of 1962.

People who knew the Armstrongs said they seemed to age overnight. How could something so terrible have happened?

For some people, talking about a tragedy helps them bear the pain. But not for Neil Armstrong. He kept the sadness to himself. He never spoke about Muffie's death then or ever. New friends often didn't realize that Neil Armstrong once had a daughter.

A week after Muffie died, Neil went back to work flying test planes. And a few months later, he made a big decision. The decision changed the rest of his life. He applied to become an astronaut.

# Chapter 5
# The Space Race

The United States' space program began in the late 1950s. Only a little more than fifty years earlier, in 1903, Wilbur and Orville Wright flew the very first airplane in Kitty Hawk, North Carolina.

Yet by mid-century, air travel was common. After the end of World War II, new planes were developed. They had jet engines. They flew at

faster and faster speeds, reaching higher and higher altitudes. Rockets were developed that could travel far into space.

In 1955, the White House announced plans to go beyond high-speed air travel. Scientists were working to launch a satellite (an unmanned craft) into space, where it would orbit Earth.

Then, on October 4, 1957, news flashed around the world. Soviet scientists had launched a satellite called *Sputnik I*. It was only the size of a beach ball and weighed less than two hundred pounds. It traveled around Earth in a little less than a hundred minutes.

The space age was born.

The space race started that same day. The goal was

the moon. Would it be the United States or the Soviet Union?

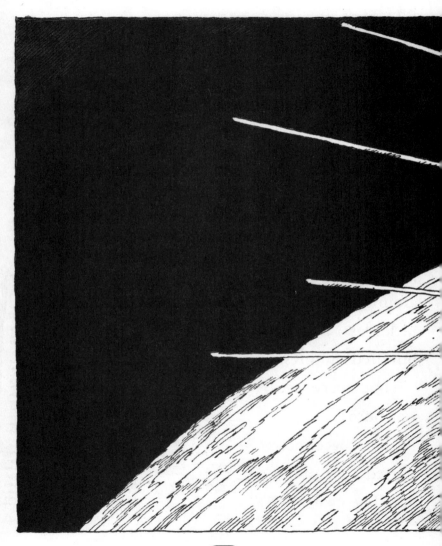

After World War II, the Soviet Union and the United States emerged as the two great super-

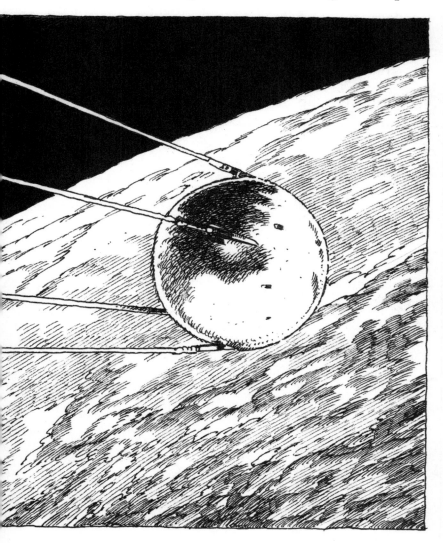

powers. They were also enemies. The Soviet Union was a Communist nation. The United States— a democracy—feared that the Soviets would force other countries to become Communist, too.

This period became known as the Cold War. There were no battles between armies. Instead,

THE SOVIET
UNION

each side built up huge storehouses of atomic bombs. The question was whether either nation would drop an atomic bomb and start World War III.

The launch of *Sputnik I* showed that Soviet technology was the most advanced in the world.

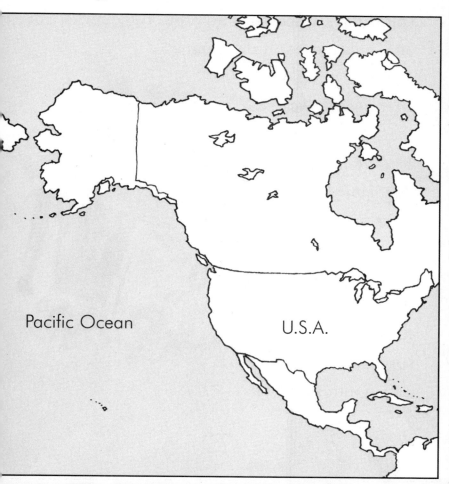

Pacific Ocean

U.S.A.

The Soviet space program was very secretive; it did not let any failures become public. Nevertheless, the Soviets had done something amazing. They'd also done it first.

Meanwhile, NASA (National Aeronautics and Space Administration) failed again and again at launching a spacecraft into orbit. (One rocket got only four inches off the ground!)

Only a month after *Sputnik I* came the much bigger *Sputnik II* with a dog named Laika as its passenger.

Then, in April 1961, the Soviets jumped even further ahead in the space race. They put a man into space. His

YURY GAGARIN

name was Yury A. Gagarin. Overnight he became world famous.

Only three weeks later, NASA sent an American test pilot named Alan Shepard soaring into space aboard a Mercury spacecraft. The flight lasted almost fifteen minutes. And Shepard piloted the vehicle himself, something Gagarin had not done.

In the United States, Shepard was given a hero's welcome upon his safe return. But in the history

ALAN SHEPARD

books, he would always remain the second human being in space. Not the first.

John F. Kennedy was president at the dawn of the space race. He took office in January of 1961. He was determined to see the United States pull ahead of the Soviets.

JOHN F. KENNEDY

The president prodded Congress to pour billions of dollars into NASA,

which was based in Houston. (Spacecraft, however, were launched from Cape Canaveral, Florida, because the area's mild weather meant launches could take place any time of year.)

A team of seven men was picked as the very first group of astronauts.

GORDON COOPER    SCOTT CARPENTER

VIRGIL GRISSOM

JOHN GLENN          DONALD SLAYTON

WALTER SCHIRRA          ALAN SHEPARD

In a famous speech before Congress, President Kennedy said, "I believe that this nation should commit itself to achieving the goal, before the decade is out, of landing a man on the moon, and returning him safely to Earth."

By the end of the decade? That meant an American astronaut had to reach the moon before 1970. To many people, that seemed an impossible dream. But the challenge had been issued. NASA would do all it could to make the dream a reality.

# THE U.S.S.R.—ALLY, THEN ENEMY

BY 1943, THE U.S.S.R.—ALSO KNOWN AS RUSSIA OR THE SOVIET UNION—WAS FIGHTING ON THE SAME SIDE AS GREAT BRITAIN AND THE UNITED STATES IN WORLD WAR II.

WHEN THE WAR ENDED IN 1945 WITH GERMANY'S DEFEAT, THE FRIENDSHIP BETWEEN THE UNITED STATES AND THE U.S.S.R. ENDED, TOO. BOTH COUNTRIES WERE VERY POWERFUL. THE UNITED STATES SAW THAT THE U.S.S.R. HOPED TO GAIN CONTROL OF OTHER COUNTRIES IN DIFFERENT PARTS OF THE WORLD. THAT WOULD MAKE THE U.S.S.R. TOO POWERFUL.

WORLD WAR II WAS OVER, BUT THE "COLD WAR" HAD BEGUN AND LASTED UNTIL THE COLLAPSE OF THE U.S.S.R. IN 1991.

WINSTON CHURCHILL    JOSEPH STALIN
FRANKLIN D. ROOSEVELT

# Chapter 6
# Astronaut Neil Armstrong

In 1962, NASA decided to bring more astronauts into the space program. NASA especially wanted test pilots and men with engineering backgrounds.

Neil Armstrong met all the qualifications. He was less than thirty-five years old, in perfect health, and shorter than six feet tall. (Taller men would be too cramped inside a small space capsule.) In addition, Neil was a highly skilled pilot *and* an engineer who knew all about the mechanics of planes and flight. Last of all, he was a man. Women were not accepted into the U.S. astronaut program until 1978. (The U.S.S.R. sent a woman cosmonaut into space in 1963.)

Neil went back and forth about whether to apply. As a test pilot, he was used to flying planes

all by himself, being in charge, and making all the decisions during a flight. As an astronaut, he would be inside a spacecraft guided mainly by automatic controls. The top engineers at the NASA command center in Houston would be in charge of every flight. But the dream of reaching the moon was a powerful one. And perhaps Neil thought a new challenge would help take his mind off the loss of his daughter. In the end, he sent in his application. It actually arrived a week after the deadline, but evidently that didn't matter to NASA. On September 17, 1962, nine men were chosen.

Neil Armstrong was one of them. And suddenly he—and the rest of his family—was famous!

The Armstrongs moved to El Lago, Texas, near the NASA space center in Houston. They had a new house that looked exactly like all the other houses in the neighborhood. It had a swimming pool in the backyard and—best of

all—air-conditioning! Summers in Texas would have been very unpleasant without it. All their neighbors were in the space program, too. There were lots of backyard barbecues with the other astronaut families. After Muffie's recent death, it was a much happier time for Neil, Jan, and their sons. (Mark Stephen Armstrong was born in the spring of 1963.)

The nine new astronauts went through a long and thorough training period. NASA had to accomplish many tasks in space before being ready to send men to the moon.

On the face of it, some of the training exercises seemed to have nothing to do with space flight. For example, soon after becoming an astronaut, Neil was sent to the steamy jungle of Panama. Why?

The reason was simple. On returning from the moon, a spacecraft might crash anywhere on Earth—a mountaintop, the desert, or the jungle. Astronauts had to be able to survive until rescued. So Neil and a fellow astronaut spent several days in the rain forest in a small tent with just a survival kit.

They ate whatever they could find—even if that meant bugs, roots, and worms!

Being an astronaut became Neil's life. It was much more than a job. According to Jan, the

Apollo mission "consumed" her husband. And the training hardly ever let up—lasting twelve or more hours a day.

In a spacecraft, there is no gravity. Everything is weightless and floats unless it is anchored down. NASA had a special plane in which Neil and the eight others could experience weightlessness for short periods of time. Its nickname was the "Vomit Comet." It would dive down from a high altitude, then climb up steeply for another dive.

It was like being on a roller coaster. At the very top of each climb, the astronauts would experience weightlessness for about thirty seconds.

Due to his demanding job, Neil spent less time at home. One night he arrived home very late. Neil hadn't been asleep for very long when both he and Jan woke up. The house was hot, very hot. And it wasn't because the air-conditioning was broken. The Armstrongs' house was on fire!

Ed White, an astronaut who lived next door, jumped over the fence between the two houses. He got out the hoses even before the fire engines arrived. No one was hurt, but the Armstrongs' house had to be rebuilt. Many photographs of little Muffie were lost in the fire as well.

Neil also had to spend a lot of time away from home giving speeches around the country. It was his least favorite part of the job. But people needed to understand the importance of the space program and why such vast amounts of money were needed for it. And of course people loved meeting the astronauts. They were young, bright, attractive men. They put a human face on the space program.

# Chapter 7
# First Voyage in Space

In March of 1966, Neil Armstrong got his first chance to put his training to the test. He was the command pilot of *Gemini 8*, which was to "dock"

or connect with another satellite already in space. This was an important step in the goal of reaching the moon. Why? NASA was designing a two-in-one spacecraft for the moon landing. A small landing device would disconnect from a larger spacecraft, touch down on the moon, and then blast off from the moon's surface and reunite with the larger craft before returning to Earth.

On *Gemini 8*, the launch was perfect and so

was the docking. Neil described it as "really a smoothie." But then things went terribly wrong. The spacecraft started spinning, just like in training sessions. Only this time it was for real.

Neil's copilot, David Scott, relayed the news to NASA officials in Houston. "We have serious problems here . . . we're tumbling end over end."

Even after *Gemini 8* separated from the satellite, it kept rolling violently, faster and faster. Both astronauts' vision began to blur. Somehow Neil managed to work the craft's hand controls. He steadied *Gemini 8*, but NASA insisted that the craft return to Earth immediately. The mission was over. David Scott would not get to "walk" in space while *Gemini 8* orbited around Earth.

The astronauts splashed down in the Pacific Ocean and were picked up, safe and sound. But newspapers criticized the mission. One called it a "nightmare in space." Afterward, Neil was very depressed about not completing the mission. He

worried that somehow he had made a mistake. Perhaps NASA would think twice before sending him on future trips into space. But it turned out that the problem was with a faulty thruster, a small rocket engine that provides forward motion. It was NASA's mistake, not Neil's.

Neil had a much closer call on May 6, 1968, during a training exercise. He was piloting a vehicle called the "flying bedstead" because it looked a little like a mattress. It had been a routine flight. Neil

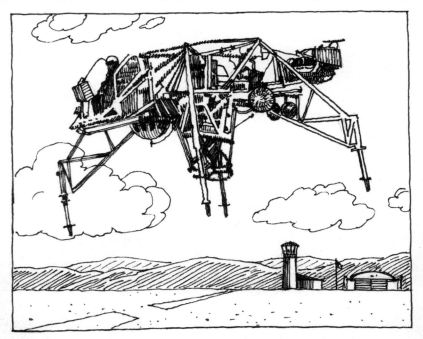

was less than two hundred feet from landing on the ground. With no warning, the flying bedstead began to spin out of control. Neil had to eject and parachute onto the runway just seconds before the plane crashed and went up in flames. The public sometimes lost sight of the risks involved in the space program. The astronauts and the scientists at NASA, however, never did. That's why the training and testing was so long and hard.

At the end of December of 1968, the *Apollo 8* astronauts orbited the moon. The purpose was to search for good landing spots. This was the next-to-last step before landing a man on the moon. The next missions were to perfect the landing device that would separate from the larger spacecraft and touch down on the surface of the moon.

In January 1969, Neil Armstrong was named commander of *Apollo 11*. The other two astronauts were Buzz Aldrin and Michael Collins. Most of the earlier Apollo crews became good friends during their many

BUZZ ALDRIN

months training together. The three men of *Apollo 11* worked well together but never grew close. It wasn't that they disliked one another, but at the end of the

MICHAEL COLLINS

day, they got in their cars and drove their separate ways. Then they'd return the next day and resume training.

They worked inside life-size models of their spacecraft and the landing device. Every step of the mission was practiced over and over. NASA engineers in Texas would control much of the flight through computers, but the astronauts were on their own if anything went wrong. Sometimes the engineers would purposely cause errors to test the skills of Neil, Buzz, and Michael.

A Saturn V rocket would launch the spacecraft named *Columbia* into orbit around Earth and then blast it in the direction of the moon. Once *Columbia* was pulled into the moon's orbit, the four-legged landing device (similar to the flying bedstead) could separate and touch down. Neil and Buzz would spend about two and a half hours on the moon while Michael stayed alone in *Columbia* orbiting the moon.

After a couple of hours on the moon, Neil and Buzz would enter the top part of the landing device and blast off. (The bottom part of the landing device would remain on the moon.) Once they reconnected with *Columbia*, the astronauts would climb back into the cabin and the return trip to Earth would begin.

That was the plan . . . but would it work?

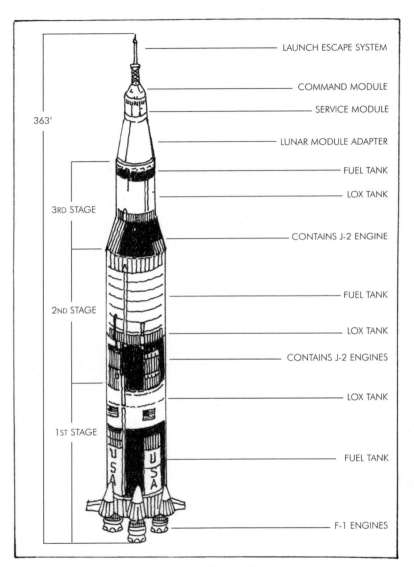

LAUNCH ESCAPE SYSTEM

COMMAND MODULE

SERVICE MODULE

LUNAR MODULE ADAPTER

FUEL TANK

LOX TANK

CONTAINS J-2 ENGINE

FUEL TANK

LOX TANK

CONTAINS J-2 ENGINES

LOX TANK

FUEL TANK

F-1 ENGINES

363'

3RD STAGE

2ND STAGE

1ST STAGE

# SATURN V

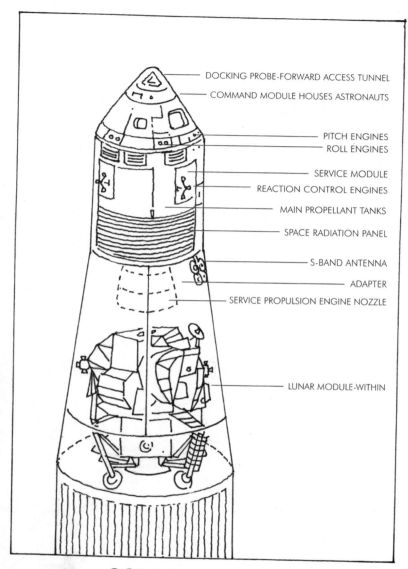

DOCKING PROBE-FORWARD ACCESS TUNNEL

COMMAND MODULE HOUSES ASTRONAUTS

PITCH ENGINES
ROLL ENGINES

SERVICE MODULE

REACTION CONTROL ENGINES

MAIN PROPELLANT TANKS

SPACE RADIATION PANEL

S-BAND ANTENNA

ADAPTER

SERVICE PROPULSION ENGINE NOZZLE

LUNAR MODULE-WITHIN

# COMMAND MODULE

# THE DANGERS OF SPACE FLIGHT

THE APOLLO PROGRAM CAME AFTER THE GEMINI PROGRAM. APOLLO SPACECRAFT WERE BIGGER AND BETTER. NASA THOUGHT A MOON LANDING MIGHT HAPPEN IN 1967.

THREE ASTRONAUTS WERE CHOSEN FOR THE FIRST APOLLO MISSION—ROGER CHAFFEE, GUS GRISSOM, AND ED WHITE, THE KIND NEIGHBOR WHO HELPED THE ARMSTRONGS

WHITE        GRISSOM        CHAFFEE

DURING THE HOUSE FIRE.

AS ALWAYS, THERE WAS A DRESS REHEARSAL A COUPLE OF WEEKS BEFORE THE ACTUAL FLIGHT. THE THREE MEN WERE IN THEIR SPACE SUITS, STRAPPED INTO THE CAPSULE THAT SAT ATOP A GIANT SATURN ROCKET. A FRAYED WIRE SENT OUT A SPARK. IN SECONDS, THE SMALL CABIN WAS ENGULFED IN FLAMES. ALL THREE ASTRONAUTS WERE KILLED ALMOST INSTANTLY.

NASA ALWAYS WORRIED THAT SOMETHING MIGHT GO WRONG DURING A SPACE MISSION AND ASTRONAUTS MIGHT DIE. BUT FOR A SMALL MISTAKE ON THE GROUND TO CAUSE SUCH A TRAGEDY SEEMED SENSELESS. FOR THE NEXT TWO YEARS, SCIENTISTS AND ENGINEERS RETHOUGHT EVERY STEP OF THE MOON LANDING. THE CONCERN FOR SAFETY MEANT A DELAY, BUT A NECESSARY ONE.

# Chapter 8
# Next Stop—the Moon

On the morning of July 16, 1969, Neil and his two fellow *Apollo 11* crewmen rose at 4:15 A.M. They had steak and eggs for breakfast, the same breakfast all astronauts had before a flight. The night before a special visitor had arrived for dinner to wish them good luck—Charles Lindbergh.

Once the astronauts were in their bulky space
suits and helmets, an elevator on the launchpad
took them up, past the Saturn rocket, to the space
capsule, *Columbia*.

The countdown for *Apollo 11* had started days ago. Now there were only a few minutes left until the launch. Launch control in Florida was responsible only for the very beginning of the flight. Once the craft cleared the launch tower, the NASA team in Houston would take over.

It was the last seconds of the countdown.

Six . . . five . . . four . . .

It seemed as if everyone watching held their breath.

Three . . . two . . . one . . .

Blastoff.

Trailing fire, the Saturn rocket with the astronauts inside the *Columbia* capsule soared into the sky. The entire cabin was rattling. But after just a few minutes, the ride grew smooth.

The Saturn V was a three-stage rocket engine. Three engines were needed because it wasn't possible to build a single engine with enough power to take the craft a quarter of a million miles away.

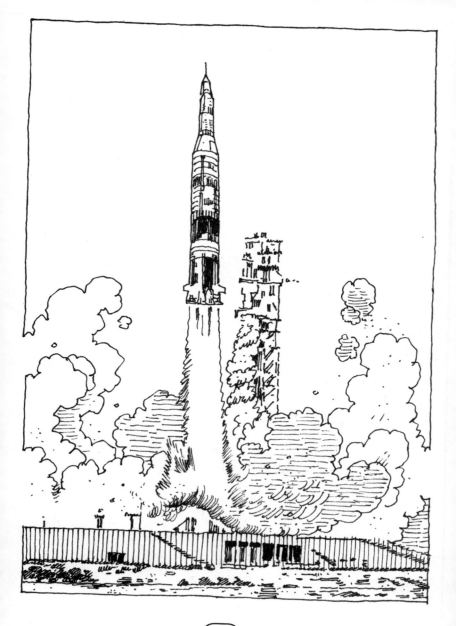

# THE JOURNEY TO THE MOON

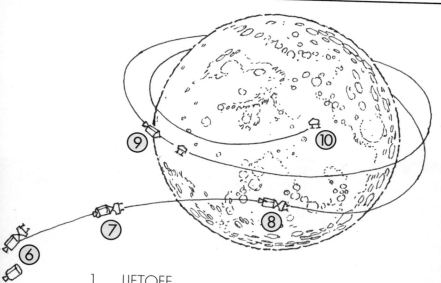

1. LIFTOFF
2. FIRST STAGE SEPARATION
3. SECOND STAGE SEPARATION
4. SEPARATION FROM LUNAR ADAPTER
5. TURNAROUND AND DOCKING
6. COMMAND MODULE AND LUNAR MODULE IN FINAL SEPARATION FROM LUNAR ADAPTER
7. MID-COURSE CORRECTION
8. LUNAR ORBIT
9. COMMAND AND LUNAR MODULE SEPARATION
10. LUNAR MODULE TOUCHDOWN

Fuel in the Saturn's first-stage engine propelled the rocket forty miles into the air. When its fuel was all used up, the first stage dropped off. At this point the second-stage engine kicked in. This took *Apollo 11* one hundred and fifteen miles above Earth.

Now the astronauts were circling Earth. After one and a half orbits, the second stage fell off and the third-stage engines fired. This sped up the *Apollo* so that it could escape Earth's gravity and continue toward the moon.

So far it had been a smooth and uneventful trip.

On the fourth morning, *Columbia* entered the moon's gravity. From this point on, every step in the mission was being done for the very first time.

After breakfast on July 20, Neil and Buzz floated from *Columbia* into the landing module, which Neil had named the *Eagle*.

"See you later," Michael Collins said to them

right before the *Eagle* separated from *Columbia*.

One and a half hours later, it was time for the *Eagle* to touch down on the moon.

The *Eagle* had to land perfectly. That meant touching down on a flat area; otherwise the *Eagle* would not be able to take off from the moon and rejoin *Columbia*. Neil and Buzz would be left stranded on the moon forever.

The landing was supposed to be controlled by computers. But as the *Eagle* got close to the moon's

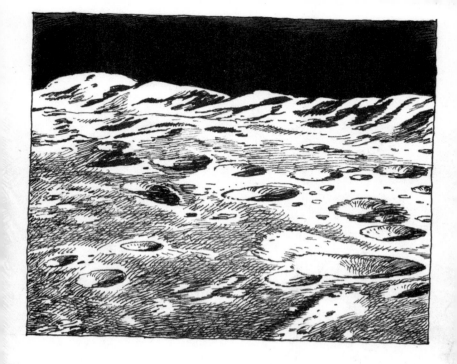

surface, Neil saw that the landing area was much too rocky.

Quickly he took the controls and looked for a safer spot. With less than a minute's worth of fuel left, he spotted a good area four and a half miles away. Then the four bug-like legs of the landing vehicle made contact with the dusty surface of the moon.

"The *Eagle* has landed!" Neil told the NASA group in Houston. Now it was time to sightsee!

# Chapter 9
# Moon Walk

Neil and Buzz could only spend two and a half hours on the moon because of the limited supply of oxygen in their tanks.

Because Neil was commander of the mission, NASA awarded him the honor of stepping onto the moon first.

Carefully Neil climbed down the ladder. He had given much thought to what he'd say. After all, his words would be heard all over the world. Neil's message was, "That's one small step for a man; one giant leap for mankind."

But as Neil set foot on the moon, four hundred and fifty million people listening heard him say, "That's one small step for man; one giant leap for mankind." Possibly Neil forgot the word *a* or else the poor sound from the moon was responsible for cutting out that one little word.

Whatever the exact words, their meaning was clear. It was indeed a landmark event in the history of the world.

Neil rigged a TV camera so viewers on Earth could watch the two men in their bulky space suits walking where no human beings had ever been before. (Their suits protected them from both the extreme heat and extreme cold on the moon.)

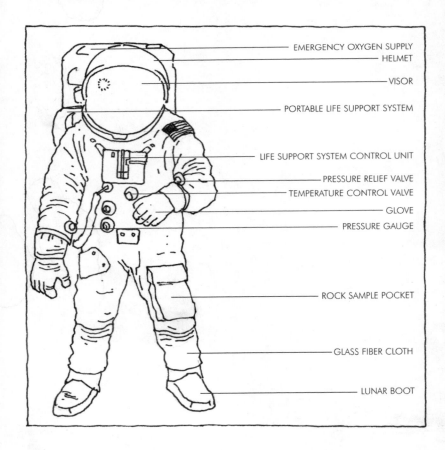

EMERGENCY OXYGEN SUPPLY
HELMET
VISOR
PORTABLE LIFE SUPPORT SYSTEM
LIFE SUPPORT SYSTEM CONTROL UNIT
PRESSURE RELIEF VALVE
TEMPERATURE CONTROL VALVE
GLOVE
PRESSURE GAUGE
ROCK SAMPLE POCKET
GLASS FIBER CLOTH
LUNAR BOOT

The astronauts collected moon rocks, took photographs, and planted an American flag. Wires made the flag look as if it were flying; otherwise it would have hung limp. (There's no wind on the moon.) And they also left a plaque. It said, "Here men from the planet Earth first set foot upon the moon July 1969 A.D. We came in peace for all mankind." Wherever they walked they left footprints in the moon dust. Those footprints are still there today! (Again because there's no wind on the moon.)

The landscape was basically brown and gray, and it was very dark out. Still, Neil thought the moon was beautiful. "Isn't that something? Magnificent sight down here," Neil said to Buzz. Both of them wished they could have stayed longer.

While Buzz and Neil were taking their tour of the moon, Mike had orbited around it fourteen times. Each time Mike was on the side of the moon that didn't face Earth, he lost communication with NASA. During that time, if a problem arose, there was no way for him to tell NASA about it. Even so, Mike later described his time alone in space as being very peaceful.

As for Neil and Buzz, everything depended on the *Eagle* blasting off perfectly from the moon's surface. Fortunately, it did. After Neil and Buzz reconnected with *Columbia*, they climbed back into the cabin with Mike. Then the *Eagle* was set adrift to orbit the moon. It had done its job. There was no need for it anymore. And besides, it couldn't be brought back to Earth. It would have burned up on hitting the atmosphere. (The *Eagle* eventually crashed into the moon.)

Once Mike fired the rockets that pulled *Columbia* away from the moon's gravity, the *Apollo 11* crewmen were on their way home!

# THE RETURN TRIP

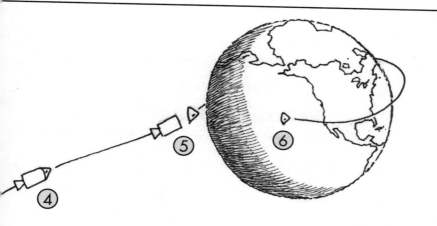

1. LUNAR MODULE LIFTS OFF
2. COMMAND AND LUNAR MODULE
   DOCK—CREW TRANSFER
3. LUNAR MODULE SEPARATES FROM
   COMMAND MODULE
4. MIDCOURSE CORRECTION
5. COMMAND AND SERVICE
   MODULE SEPARATE
6. SPLASH-DOWN AND RECOVERY

# Chapter 10
# Returning Home

It was a sixty-hour trip back to Earth. On July 24, around noon, the spacecraft pierced through the atmosphere. Three parachutes billowed out and set the craft down gently in the Pacific Ocean. A helicopter picked up the astronauts and took them to a recovery ship.

Neil, Buzz, and Mike were home.

Yes, they were finally home. But they could not see their families or friends. For almost three weeks, the three astronauts were kept in isolation. Scientists had to make sure that they had not brought back germs from the moon.

On August 13, the three astronauts and their families arrived in New York City on *Air Force One*, the president's plane. All during the parade in their honor, the cheering never stopped. People threw so much confetti and ticker tape, it looked as if there were a summertime blizzard!

Neil and his crewmates not only toured the

United States, they visited twenty-one other countries on what was called the Giant Leap Tour. The *Apollo 11* astronauts were world famous, Neil Armstrong most of all.

Neil had never liked attention. He was happiest soaring above Earth, flying in a plane. In the years after his trip to the moon, he has tried to live a much quieter life.

He became a professor at a college in Ohio. He bought a farm. Sadly, he and Janet were divorced after thirty-eight years of marriage. Neil got married again to a woman named Carol Held Knight, who also enjoys flying.

During the years of the Apollo space program, which ended in 1972, ten other astronauts walked on the moon. NASA does not have plans to send more people to the moon. And at present there is no plan to land on Mars, the closest planet to Earth. The space program is concentrating on learning more about deep space beyond our solar system.

Yet the first trip to the moon remains an important event, a great human achievement. It was, as Neil said, a "giant leap for mankind."

# TIMELINE OF NEIL ARMSTRONG'S LIFE

**1930** —— Neil Armstrong is born

**1936** —— Neil has his first ride in an airplane

**1947** —— Neil enters Purdue University

**1950** —— Neil flies war planes off the USS *Essex* during the Korean War

**1955** —— Neil marries Janet Shearon

**1957** —— Son Eric is born

**1959** —— Daughter Karen is born

**1962** —— Karen dies
Neil is accepted into the second group of nine astronauts

**1963** —— Son Mark is born

**1966** —— Neil has his first flight into space on *Gemini 8*

**1969** —— As commander of *Apollo 11*, Neil becomes the first man on the moon

**1970** —— Neil leaves NASA program

**1971** —— Neil begins teaching at the University of Cincinnati

**1994** —— Neil and Jan are divorced

**1994** —— Neil marries Carol Held Knight

# TIMELINE OF THE WORLD

| | |
|---|---|
| Charles Lindbergh makes first transatlantic flight, from Long Island to Paris | 1927 |
| The stock market crashes, triggering the Great Depression of the 1930s | 1929 |
| Adolf Hitler becomes chancellor of Nazi Germany | 1933 |
| World War II begins after Hitler's forces invade Poland | 1939 |
| After the Japanese bomb Pearl Harbor in Hawaii, the U.S. joins the war | 1941 |
| World War II ends | 1945 |
| The Cold War between the U.S. and the U.S.S.R. begins | 1957 |
| *Sputnik I* is launched into space by the U.S.S.R. | 1960 |
| Martin Luther King Jr. makes his "I Have a Dream" speech at the civil rights march on Washington, D.C. President John F. Kennedy is assassinated in Dallas | 1963 |
| Beatlemania hits the U.S. | 1964 |
| The country becomes more divided over the Vietnam War | 1967 |
| Martin Luther King Jr. is assassinated in April Robert F. Kennedy is assassinated in June | 1968 |
| The Woodstock rock music festival goes on for three days in August | 1969 |

# BIBLIOGRAPHY

Bredeson, Carmen. **Neil Armstrong: A Space Biography.** New Jersey: Enslow Publishers, 1998.

Dunham, Montrew. **Neil Armstrong: Young Flyers.** New York: Aladdin, 1996.

Fraser, Mary Ann. **One Giant Leap.** New York: Henry Holt & Company, 1993.

Hansen, James R. **First Man: The Life of Neil A. Armstrong.** New York: Simon & Schuster, 2005.

Hehner, Barbara. **First on the Moon.** New York: Hyperion Books for Children, 1999.

Kramer, Barbara. **Neil Armstrong: The First Man on the Moon.** New Jersey: Enslow Publishers, 1997.

Westman, Paul. **Neil Armstrong: Space Pioneer.** Minneapolis: Lerner Publications, 1980.

Zemlicka, Shannon. **Neil Armstrong.** New York: Barnes & Noble, 2002.